Proximidad

PROXIMIDAD
A Mexican/American Memoir

Broadstone

Broadstone Books
An Imprint of
Broadstone Media LLC
418 Ann Street
Frankfort, KY 40601-1929
BroadstoneBooks.com

Contents

Proximity

He's a guy sitting alone in a restaurant. I've met dozens like him, just as brown, who never once set foot in Mexico—they were raised someplace like Longview and spoke with that same East Texas drawl as the proudest redneck—hell, some summers I've been as brown as this man now two tables over.

I haven't heard his voice, but I've become certain he's from the other side of the fence. He glances as my wife takes our daughter to the restroom. The look lasts a half-second longer than I'd like, my head is swamped again by the research for this damn poem—all the dead and tortured girls, bodies mangled and strung, missing daughters, sex trades.

I'm such an idiot. Why did I bring them here? I want to believe that people are okay. I know I'm being unrealistic. He probably works at a fracking site nearby, all day in the sun. I know I'm profiling him, becoming what's wrong with us. I want to see him as an average, boring man. But there's too much at stake.

He's become something else: no longer exactly a guy eating alone in a cafe in Van Horn, Texas— now an opportunist on hunt for a healthy white girl to hoist over the line into Mexico and sell or keep as a toy for himself.

He pays no attention as we eat— I'm unable to let him out of my peripheral vision—not that I could do anything if he were to spring. I'm powerless.

Nothing happens. Nothing ever happens.

I teach class, tutor, joke with friends, play with
my infant daughter — always, images of the dead
rolling at the base of my skull, just beneath the
moment. Three men's heads left on the curb, a
pile of indeterminate body parts, mutilated
women strung up on wires, a loose pile of
corpses in an otherwise empty room, a woman's
desiccated and punctured face.

I change my daughter's diapers, I feed her
breakfast, she leaves me in constant swoon. A
video of a man shot in the gut, begging for help.
No one approaches to help; it's too dangerous.
They've all heard the stories of assassins
returning to finish the job, of doctors targeted
for saving gunshot victims.[1]

I find out that an old friend, a former supervisor,
is a convicted sex offender. Aggravated sexual
assault against a 7-year-old girl. He meets my
daughter when she is six months old. He acts
like she isn't there.

When Amado Carrillo takes control of Mexico's cocaine trade in the late 80's, he makes it nearly impossible to deal drugs in Juárez. Dealers are taken care of swiftly. There could be thousands of kilos of cocaine stored in Juárez, but if you want to party, you have to head into El Paso.[2]

Originally, I set out to document the horrors being inflicted on the women of Juárez. Their faces and stories keep me up late nights, open a constant hollow in my chest. And then I find out about the men: thousands mutilated, murdered. Some are obviously connected to the drug trade; others are mysteries: journalists, police, children. Drug addicts waiting in rehab cots. College students.

In 1997, Amado Carrillo dies, creating a power vacuum at the top of Mexico's drug empire and opening Juárez to its own domestic trade. Within a decade, Juárez becomes one of the most dangerous cities in the world as rival cartels battle for control of the border crossing.

After almost 20 years away, I move back to El Paso as the drug war nears its apex. We have no fear of our new hometown, consistently ranked second safest in the United States. We move into my father's house, within walking distance of the border.

open the lid on a bottle of sand

Attending grade school with children who
barely speak English. They quietly converse
with each other in their Latin and strictly un-
American tones, absorbing reprimands for
avoiding English.

> regardless what else we visualize
> *cool water laps at my thighs, we are*
> *at peace in a vast field of green grasses*

They tend toward clustering together at
playgrounds and parks. We never shy away
exactly, but we don't engage them either. They
have their own multi-tongued cliques, chartered
in Spanglish. We degrade them for their English,
sometimes to their faces: *beaner, wetback* — their
linguistic limits which sound so much like
stupidity. They remind me of my grandmother,
her English broken at its best. I wouldn't say
these things within earshot of her.

> no matter our affirmations, the self-lies
> *this reality is illusion, we are*
> *spiritual beings having a human experience*

They are the children of well-to-do Mexican
citizens, their mothers having driven them
across the bridge, braved the workers with and
without visas, the early bird tourists — to get
over here and see if an American parochial
education will allow for something better than
their nearest alternatives.

> it will always soil the shiny

Partitions

we sit in circles and discuss
   the worth of art:
   the ghost of hunger,
      boredom, loneliness —

   our voices whisper
   themselves into corners
      under desks.

the debate heats, people spin
   their cell phones,
   at least one
      shuts himself

   off into Facebook. none can
   agree how
      art best operates —

      we leave an empty water bottle

A copy of *I Live Here* is handed around the room.
I take a long pause while looking over artwork
that depicts femicide, murder, the drug war,
what's eating Juárez from the inside. There are
sections about three other areas of the world; I
am compelled to ignore them. I can't not look
away from the book about Juárez. I don't want
this information, this conveyed experience.

I flip through the book on Juárez, but four times
I return to the same page — a 3-dimensional
representation in yarn: a hairy and overweight
man reclines on a couch smoking a cigarette, a
slight trail of cotton smoke rises toward the
invisible ceiling, beer cans litter the floor, the
man holds his free hand over the head of a small
child pressed against his crotch, jeans unzipped
and pulled away, the child a quarter the size of
the man.

The image imprints itself onto me. I think about
my daughter waiting for me at home, not old
enough to know that she's waiting, my child a
quarter the size of me at most. For two years I
struggle to get the yarn image out of my head. It
never leaves; it gets a little hazier.

can these be principled lives?

force
my face into pages
label the moments

the bodies
adrift
in sand

can I be done   with stillness?

this thin scrap

of water   shielding me

drain my   cup
crumple it
for someone else

cheap
disposable

it's not a
good thing

to be concerned

In 1994, NAFTA passes and opens Mexico to an unprecedented level of trade with the United States. The maquiladora industry launches, promising good wages to thousands of Mexicans who have little to no income and little to no education. Mexico begins to import staple foods, dislocating millions of farmers and small business owners.[3]

Tens of thousands funnel into Juárez to find work; all of their families must be fed.

Shiny

an abandoned
sandbox

burden of

bodies
try to

shoulder a

conscience

insomnia

ten fingerprints

breath

just   belongings

the path
to the lungs

an empty parcel

inhale

In November 2011, my daughter drops from her mother's body and into my arms, onto our bed. The next morning, I bring her outside my father's El Paso home, naked for a short sunbath, one minute for each day she's alive. My father's house was built near the ridgeline, and I can see for at least thirty miles, probably eighty on a clear day.

In the distance, across the street, between two houses, the view over downtown and into Juárez. Six or seven people will be killed in Juárez within twenty-four hours of my daughter's first contact with the sun. Tomorrow, I will repeat the sunbath and add a minute; six extra dead bodies, maybe more.[4]

At least once a week we would go into Juárez to buy gas or groceries, or to visit the old market. And, of course, we'd visit my mother's parents.

On the way home, we would stop by our favorite panadería. They always had an assortment of pastries, and I usually snagged a couple, perusing the shelves with a set of tongs and a plastic tray; but the real treat of the night was getting a load of freshly baked bolillos which were always cooking.

Depending on how busy the store was at the time, the bolillo basket might be swamped with patrons trying to get their hands on some freshly baked bread. Either my father or mother braved the mob to get us a half dozen or more steaming rolls.

Almost always, on our way out the door, sitting against the walls of the shopping center, moving from one person to us, their eyes lighting up as a potential new source of income approached, the broken of Juárez. We quickly made our way from the door to the car; none but us would get this fresh bread.

I don't know if it was some kind of survival instinct or habit that told us to get food for the way home. Whatever it was, we had something to eat while we made our way home — the 3-mile journey could take hours.

El Paso and Juárez are separated by a leak in the Earth we call the Rio Grande. The line of cars crossing into El Paso sometimes stretched a half mile or more, occasionally passing the Parque Público Federal Chamizal, the sister to the Chamizal Park directly across the river in El Paso, symbols of peace and prosperity between these two neighboring countries.

When the line was particularly long, we took another snail's pace tour of the park's outskirts while we waited in bumper-to-bumper traffic to get to the bridge.

I was never taught much about poverty; it was a fact of life on the border. The Juárez shanties that peppered the hillside in sight of the university, whole families sharing less space than that in which my family ate dinner—we were middle class at best, but we had more than enough space. Those other "homes" were nothing more than boxes on a hill, decorations, undiscussed.

The rise up to the top of the bridge was filled with five lanes' worth of vehicles, and a share of Mexican pedestrians carving out something like a living—selling all manner of things: snacks—refreshments if they could afford a cart or cooler. And there were always the beggars, walking from car to car with hands outstretched, hopeful for a bit of currency.

We made no eye contact—my wife would learn about this many years later on our sole trip into Juárez together. She looked a man in the eye, signaling to him that she was interested in buying his snacks; he came right to the car, and cursed us when we refused to open the window. That was the summer of 2007, a few weeks before the city was to erupt into the worst sprees of violence it had ever known.

My family lived in an El Paso neighborhood, distant enough from downtown and the border crossings that poverty wasn't a feature of our everyday life. My mother's parents lived in the Juárez house she grew up in, an upper-middle class neighborhood among la gente bien.

When my parents took us downtown to the old market, we would see—on the sidewalks, wandering outside shops, lying on cardboard or old blankets—people, mostly ignored. They would sometimes reach a thin hand out in supplication, but many of them just watched, resigned as everyone else passed by with their money. There too, we avoided eye contact — somehow they would eat. We weren't taught to look away; doing so was simply more convenient.

a delusion: no innocents
no crossfire

what if I refuse to believe the stories

a 17-year-old
a doctor
a pile

I walk
dead on the street

masked police

with his son   the journalist
slumped over

his son's arm   missing
dead

well after

I could buy dozens of guns
            because of my blank record

                        fill my trunk with an arsenal

                        quadruple what I spent

            it is near impossible to buy guns in Mexico

desperation best operates inside

the proposal:

    stock the kitchen
    dress my girl

                        bear   the report
    of a body found riddled and strung
    drowned   in border business

muchacho
muchacho   muchacho

grandfather's word
reserved for his first
                    grandson

        tato

            my brother's babyish
pronunciation

abuela   devolved

                    bela

I am born into a border world
readymade with these epithets

        tato

                                    bela

my mother
                    becomes   slowly

        abuelita

my daughter's gift of mispronunciation   li-li
                                        li-li
                                    li-li

There is an American belief that all people who
immigrate or descend from the 21 distinctly
different progenies of Hispania are

culturally alike,
vote as a group,
  dance salsa, speak Spanish

or Portuguese, can't cut it

  in the schools, work in menial
  jobs, join gangs, look
  alike, think alike, prefer
  to be separated from
"Anglo" America, and have

    "You're what?! Yeah
  sure: Ed O'Casey
    the Hispanic."

no heritage.[5]

Fortification

bulletproof   in Mexico
   a bridge in Juárez
   named after my grandfather

I'm the last person who'd be arrested   too timid

   my only   Mexican funeral
   his cancer

      across the river
      haphazardly shacks
      a landscape

         what comes next?

My mother is raised by her Mexican parents in Juárez. My brother and I grow up with one foot in Juárez. Once a week or more, we cross the hump of the bridge into Mexico to visit family, to buy food and handmade goods, to wade through Saturday night crowds of young men and women pooled together for the cheapest party available.

We celebrate Christmas, sometimes Halloween with the Mexican half of the family. At New Years, we gather at my uncle's house—when midnight hits, we fire pistols at the sky, the neighborhood air transforms into a rattle of gunshots.

Everyone in my high school knows that if you want to get the best weed, you get the shit that comes from just across the river. But I don't know anyone who actually buys their weed in Juárez, even the friends I have who live across the border. Everyone has connections in El Paso. They all say it's Mexican weed, but no one really seems to know.

She peeks out a window. The body of her husband
sits upright in his car seat. It is a professional hit.

Three bullet holes through the windshield,
as close together as the knuckles on a hand,
three more through the driver's window.

Eventually a patrol car pulls up.
But the dispatcher never sends an ambulance.[6]

insulated   from manufactured

stressors

worry   was
    a wallet lifted
        cash
        cards
        ID

            the picture
                my grandfather

who even carries cash anymore

        cancel the cards

        everything else
                        backed up online

no risk
    but

        injury   sickness
            the body   diet

        death and dismemberment
                accidents

        metamorphosis
            a warning for
            the next hopeful

She's the administrative director of the Juárez police.
She lives in a very nice neighborhood, and at about
10:23pm on Monday, June 16, she is murdered in
front of her house. A sign thoughtfully left with her
corpse explains that she had hired too many people
associated with El Chapo Guzmán.
Her name is Sylvia Guzmán Molina.
Before her murder, she was law enforcement, and by
the standard of the city, an innocent. But having
been assassinated, she now becomes dirty, someone
who must have been connected to bad people
doing bad things.[7]

junkies

in rehabs   meetings

taken care of

5 years away
                    nine in   rehab
church service

                    undecorated

detox   waiting room

          delirium
tremens
                    the harvest

4 years
     a memory

          two rehabs

          twenty-eight
          addicted no longer

another family shrunken

supplications shaking at the sun
    begging for
    what?

            a stem to the tide
            a slower march
            for Santa Muerte

a dry empty and welcoming
pine box

is this how prayer operates?

    increasing
    consciousness
    of the absent

something rushes   to fill
          silence

they pile loose dirt high over the coffin

the Principle of Scarring:

    he'll be in there
             forever

machinations of   soil,

    the laws of force   applied

this now nameless
                sprouting

Two bodies were seen hanging from a pedestrian bridge. A
message was left on a banner next to the bodies and was
signed by the Gulf Cartel (CDG). The victims were both
young girls ages 15 and 16 and had been reported missing
since November 20. They were held by members of CDG
in order to gather information on Los Zetas. Both
of the victims were known to associate with members
of organized crime. The bodies were
hanging from yellow plastic chords.

"Mexico starts in Juárez!"
the billboard reads — I pass it every day
during my commute.
If this is its beginning,
where is the end?

One of the messages on the banner read,
"Fucking Z Juan Bandido don't be a faggot,
confront us whore, come and pick up your trash.
Respond for your people, don't be a coward."[8]

In Mexico, 98% of murders go unpunished. This is a derivation of another statistic: in only 2% of murders in Mexico is someone convicted.[9]

Next to the doughnuts in the middle of the table — fingerprints in the dust that coats the platter's rim. With the resources at most police departments, I could identify each person who's taken one of these treats.

From 2007 to 2013, more than 11,000 people are murdered in Juárez. In that same period, between 120,000 and 130,000 people are killed in all of Mexico. An additional 25,000-plus people disappear in that time.[10]

Four of the six people killed in Juárez on April 16, 2012 are women. Two are killed in a drive-by shooting; one is shot to death; a few blocks away, another, a 17-year-old girl, is shot to death while taking care of a baby.[11]

From 1993 to 1997, the murder rate for women in Juárez increases 600% over the previous five years. The mainstream press teems with articles and commentary about *femicide* and the mysterious lack of perpetrators.

In that same time period, men still manage to account for 90% of the murder victims in Juárez.[12] Men are tortured, strangled, mutilated, cooked in vats of boiling water — their heads and extremities are found all over the city.[13]

Just about every time a woman in Juárez is killed, it's labelled a femicide, regardless of the circumstances of her death.[14]

On January 23, 1993, the body of 13-year-old Alma Chavira Farrel is found. She was strangled and beaten, raped anally and vaginally. Had she grown old and died, I never would have learned her name.

No special label is applied when a man is killed.

el 22 de Septiembre

Cuerpo A: Masculino no identificado,
de entre 20 y 25 años

Cuerpo B: Masculino no identificado,
de entre 40 y 45 años

Cuerpo C: Masculino no identificado,
de entre 20 y 25 años

Cuerpo D: Femenina no identificada,
de entre 30 y 35 años

Cuerpo E: Femenina no identificada,
de entre 5 y 10 años

Cuerpo F: Masculino no identificado,
de entre 25 y 30 años

Cuerpo G: Masculino no identificado,
de entre 20 y 25 años

Cuerpo H: Masculino no identificado,
de entre 25 y 30 años

Cuerpo I: Masculino no identificado,
de entre 45 y 50 años

Cuerpo J: Masculino no identificado,
de entre 30 y 35 años[15]

At 2:00pm Monday, two human heads were
found on a bridge. They had been placed in
two tubs with hominy, vegetables, and other
ingredients used to cook and accompany the
traditional Mexican dish pozole. Also included
were tostadas, hot sauce, two bottles of Coca-

> *Fill half a bin with*
> *200 liters of water. Add*
> *two sacks of caustic soda.*

Cola, paper plates, and spoons. The heads were
set out in the sun with cigarettes in their mouths.

> *Put it on the fire*
> *and boil it. Place the human*
> *remains in the bin,*

Hacerlos pozole is an expression used by narcos

> *leaving them at least eight hours.*
> *Once only the liquid is left*
> *along with the teeth and nails*
> *allow it to cool.*

to refer to the procedure employed when bodies
of those linked to organized crime are dissolved
in drums with acid. Santiago Meza López was
one of the FBI's 20 most wanted criminals. He

> *Empty the contents into another*
> *plastic bin. Take that to a vacant lot,*
> *preferably one littered with*
> *garbage. Throw gasoline on*

> *everything, set fire to it all.*

was known as "The Stew Maker," El Pozolero.
"I felt nothing. I just disposed of the bodies by
dipping them in acid."[16]

in a brick oven
burned alongside
seven tires

inside a 200-liter vat
corrosive acid
hands and feet remain

face down
skeletal remains

pink jacket [17]

New Ghosts

I take regular naps with our infant daughter. She gets tired in the middle of the day when I'm usually home. I pick her up, and she rests her head on my shoulder. I quietly sing Ween's version of "The Unquiet Grave" as her cheek slides down to my chest, and her eyes slowly float closed. Sometimes the walk is long, and my shoulders and arms ache from the effort of holding her twenty pounds in the same position, of walking as gently and steadily as I can. I'm trying to simulate life in the womb — warmth, the cradle of one step after another — where she first learned to sleep.

I sit on the couch, maybe turn on the TV muted; she sleeps peacefully atop me, and sometimes, to be honest, I drift off as well. Other times, I consider what's happening to some of the infants living across the dry river bed of the Rio Grande, almost in sight of where we live; I don't believe in owning a gun, I am tempted.

                                    1999
            no drug-   related

            murders in Juárez

      for the   new governor

one murder-free year:
                                 a gift

      the years since:
                        a message

Maria de Jesus Bilbao says that every night she talks with her son Israel who was assassinated in March 2008 at the age of 18. She says when she lies down at night, she feels his presence at the foot of the bed. He is dressed in white. She asks who it was that hurt him, and Israel places his index finger to his mouth and says he can't tell her.[18]

are women
        commodities   until they fight

can't wash

    work clothes

    with   the family's

        new son born   without

        a brain

    children   trained

        slurry-soaked groundwater

           makeshift   electric lines

        lie on the ground

    houses   discarded garage

        doors

    amperes certain as buckshot[19]

*Hanes Blooming Beauty. Our comfort-fit
promise ensures feel-good wear. Brief styling
offers full coverage. Elastic waistband promises
pull-on/pull-off ease.*

*SmartWool Microweight Hiphugger. Not
the itchy bulky wool you're thinking of.
Midrise, athletic brief provides a little more
coverage, yet still hugs your curves.*

*Fruit of the Loom Mesh Thong Panties. Elastic
waist. Bold colors in a breathable and flirty mesh
design will soon make these panties
your all-time favorite.*

*Hanes Plus Cotton Women's Brief. Wide
elastic no-tag waist stretches gently for
all-day ease. Classic brief cut gives full
coverage, front and back. Finally, panties
that don't misbehave.*

*Vanishing Edge Microfiber Boyshort. Make
panty lines disappear forever. Provides
breathable stay-put silicone at the leg openings
for a no-show look and no-ride fit.*

*Cosabella Talco G-String. Uncover ultra
soft and comfortable wear. Buttery soft
jersey fabric babies the skin.
Hand wash – hang dry.*[20]

With NAFTA, the price of corn in Mexico dropped 70%.

American corn farmers can sell their crop below cost.

The Mexican corn farmer lost 70% of his profit in a moment:

Illegal immigrants make a handsome wage picking corn

70 of the 100 square feet of his house, 1.4 chickens,

compared to their Mexican counterparts.

1½ of his children, 29% of his daughter's virginity,

The United States is Mexico's number 1 importer of corn.

3 of every 4 days' worth of *honor, obey, 'til death do us,* etc.[21]

Mexico's
leper hand

fingers crumble
            to a pale
carry

nightspots   American

El Paso's   drinking

                    mouth

        sticks
            her tongue

                wonders at a new
        color   infection

her lips nuzzle   writhe

lines have been painted, banners
stitched together to stretch across
downtown streets and the auditorium.

if the purpose of charity work is résumé boosting,
the meek shall inherit the earth, laden
in leaded clay, criss-crossed with slurry rivers.

the parade balloons have fallen,
paint spots on the colonias.

the meek caught   in the act of inheritance
the incumbents and their McMansions
their luxury   the boulevards

the managers drive over the hump
at the river, witness to the fiesta:

children sell gum and snacks,
limbless men navigate
bumpers, crates hoisted over
the side into the waiting trunks
of mules, the endless exchange
of sugar and rusted fingernails

What are the advantages of the maquiladora program?

Low labor costs.
Trainable workforce.

Low labor costs.
Proximity to U.S. market
and distribution centers.

Low labor costs.

Cooperative, predominantly
nonunion workforce.

Low   labor costs. Fine quality
of life for U.S. managers
living in El Paso. Low labor

costs.   Sophisticated

transportation infrastructure.

Low labor costs. Experienced
Mexican technicians and

supervisors. Low labor costs.

World-class production facilities.[22]

let's go over what should have been learned
before applying for this job:

the First Law of Economics:

a k of H is 23K.

the Original Law of Thermoeconomics:

the amount of heat applied to a given
system = skin + corruption.

The total heat that can be applied
is a constant derived from the proportion
of blood to mean income.

the Only Law of Cardioeconomics:
demand is ever present—

one need only supply sufficient friction.

the Principle Law of Narcoeconomics:

there is no negotiation.

you pay what's on the tag. Always.

The dilemma of plata o plomo? (silver or lead) —
accept the bribe or the bullet — weighs heavily on
Mexican civil servants, law enforcement officials,
and security forces. Even high-ranking federal
officials and military personnel are not immune;

>   I wasn't old enough to buy beer —
> pot was much easier to get.
> We fogged out the car on the way
>   from the Westside to the Lower Valley,
>   not even a mile from the river. I stuffed

>   myself with pizza, considered Xanax,
> and stood with a thousand El Pasoans, singing
> along with Three Dog Night:
>   Joy to the world.
>   All the boys and girls.

in the past decade, two of Mexico's antidrug chiefs
have been arrested for taking payoffs from drug
kingpins, and the trafficking organization Los Zetas
owes its infamous origins to assistance from corrupt
former military personnel.[23]

it takes more than an hour to open this bank account

there is no silverware left on the salad bar
we pick at the dressing and greens
    while we wait

    I enjoy *Weeds*   *Breaking Bad*
    The Wire   I cheer for the big sale
    take pride in their success

    dissolve bodies   stockpile weaponry
        drink from the cup   life extinguished

    I laugh with them under

all the groceries are
away, the fridge is full again —
what remains in these plastic bags:
the bags only

Shortly after midnight Sunday, the bodies of two
men were found inside six plastic bags in a Ford
Windstar at a convenience store on Boulevard
Juan Pablo II in northeast Juárez.

filled with each other
they take shelves in the pantry — we promise
to reuse them,   this kind of plastic that can't be
recycled that will never
totally break down

The van had been reported stolen earlier this month.[24]

The Honorable Guest List

your dollar   at least
        an industry

participants and
        bystanders   before

or after strangulation

a variety of Mexican
            and American
            prostitutes

dollar bills

worn dirt paths
                that smell
            faintly   of weed

            the wringing of hands   and their lost
                fingers

well-trained assassins and
        torturewives
            and the poorly trained

        bullets
            spent   and unspent

        fifties and hundreds

heat and water
        denied the colonias

        stolen cars   and safehouses

vats of lime   waiting
        for human meal

twos and fives

all the nostril
you ever wanted

that joint   you smoked at the prom

the heroin in that X

the night we snuck out and bought

a sweaty 8-ball
even though we got shaky
and flushed it

the complicit sewer pipes

thousands
thousands

trafficking

40% of its GDP

thousands

pesos   like sand

Proximity

three people shot
off-duty federal agents
at the Chamizal

names unreleased
no shots or injuries on the U.S. side

cross-border traffic stopped
for 20 minutes at the bridge
except tractor-trailer rig traffic

appropriate actions

Luz Maria Dávila stood in the Cibeles
Convention Center, face to face with
President Felipe Calderón:

I will not shake your hand. You are not my friend.
You are not welcome here. This Ferriz and this
Baeza, they always say the same things, but they
don't do anything. All I have are two dead sons.

Pecan trees emerging from holes
in the Juárez sidewalk. Their white-washed
trunks feel of winter — alone, I stare
through the bare branches
at the pale sky above.

My jacket stays zipped closed, the air
nips at me — two blocks from my
grandfather's house.

I want you to apologize for what you said, that
they were gangsters. It's a lie! They were not
hanging out in the streets! They were studying
and working. Here in Juárez for two years these
people have been committing these murders and
they have been committing other crimes and no
one does anything about it.

Do something! If it were you who had your
son murdered, you wouldn't leave any stone
unturned looking for the killers, but since I
don't have any resources, I am not able to look.

Her speech destroyed what was still
left of the decorum of the President's
four-hour meeting.[26]

Sunday morning   the familial mix
of chatter and laugh

those who want coffee
        have it

    everyone in polished shoes
        stomachs fed

        minds rested

no fear someone
    will drop the door in

    no fear the shock

        and peal
            of Glock

        will intersect the conversation

    no fear of disappearing

                bound at the extremes
            of the imminent grave

cars parked outside glint in the recent risen sun
moisture evacuates the ground   the bowing
of heads in gentle supplication   to a power greater

Poetry is the anti-spectacle.
It's hard to trust yourself with this silence

on the page. No such thing as objectivity –
your influence and privilege are involved.

On the way into El Paso, a full-size
pickup — no plates, hand-drawn dealer
tags, a leftover bullet hole in the front
        windshield eye-level — who
        was lucky enough to trade it in?

Don't presume too much about your objectivity.
Thinking is already engaging with

a topic. Get to some place uncomfortable
and listen. Translation isn't even

the same genre as the original.
The angle of perception is critical.[27]

A group of protesters set fire to the wooden door of Mexican president Enrique Peña Nieto's ceremonial palace in Mexico City's historic city center late on Saturday, denouncing the apparent massacre of forty-three trainee teachers.

The group, carrying torches, broke away from what had been a mostly peaceful protest demanding justice for the students, who were abducted six weeks ago and apparently murdered and incinerated by corrupt police in league with drug gang members.[28]

scant details

a culvert near

just this side of the border

       burned body

      autopsy

   to identify

I see El Pozolero dragged
away in cuffs, piles

of weaponry, rehab

   walls wiped quickly clean

reports of smoke

      dousing

     more remains[29]

there must be

gods

in contention here

cardboard
schools   coke-stained

dollars   Santa Muerte

her
strokes

of blood

narcos   the
real
prophets

messages   written in dismemberment

the worst orphanage

its waiting list

Just before 7 a.m. on Saturday, dozens of soldiers
and police officers descended on a condominium
tower in Mazatlán, Mexico, a beach resort known

I'm in Van Horn, Texas, racially
profiling my own people.
A Hispanic man sits on his own
　　　　at a table near us, eyeing my wife
　　　　and daughter. My lungs tighten

　　　　with adrenaline as I wait for him
to pull a gun and run
off with my little girl.
　　　　He calmly eats his supper.

as much as a hangout for drug traffickers as for
its seafood and surf. The forces were following yet
another tip about the whereabouts of one of the
world's most wanted drug kingpins, Joaquín Guzmán
Loera — known as El Chapo, which means "Shorty."

Mexican marines and the police, aided by
information from the DEA, immigration
and customs officials, and U.S. Marshals,
took him into custody without firing a shot.[30]

76

During the last five years the border has been shocked
by a series of 25 massacres. The first of these events
took place at a rehabilitation center for drug addicts
in 2008. Even though the level of violence has declined
in Juárez, uncertainty remains. "We're used to this; we

Test-driving my new bike
in downtown El Paso, nighttime, well-lit.
The air suffused with particles of burning
        tire from across the river—it's going
to be a cold night.

expected it because we haven't swallowed the story that
the violence is over. We knew that sooner or later there
would be another massacre because violence always
manifests itself here."[31]

Acknowledgments

I would like to extend gratitude to the editors of these journals, literary magazines, and anthologies: *Berkeley Poetry Review, Consequence, Outrage: A Protest Anthology for Injustice in a Post 9/11 World, pacificRE-VIEW, Pine Hills Review, Rio Grande Review, The Thing Itself, and Writer's Bloc.* Several poems from this collection appeared in these publications in some form or other.

I also offer thanks and love to my wife and daughter, without whom this book would have been highly improbable. Their patience and motivation allowed me the level of introspection required to bring these thoughts to fruition.

This book would never have become what it is without the effort, feedback, and insight of Carmen Gimenez-Smith, Richard Greenfield, Jennifer Eldridge, Paul French, Laura Terry, and Carrie Tafoya. I would be remiss if I trivialized the help I've received from Taylor Collier, Octavio Quintanilla, Justin Irizarry, Bruce Bond, Corey Marks, Lily Hoang, Connie Voisine, Jeff Pickell, and Patrick Lee Clark. Their remarks have shaped the arc of my work over these past few years.

I am thankful to Broadstone Books, and especially Larry Moore for his faith in my work as well as the amount of time and courtesy he extended to me throughout the entire process.

And finally, I thank my father Tom, mother Vicky, brother Sean, grandmothers and grandfathers Mexican and Irish, and all the uncounted whose shoulders I must unfortunately stand upon.

Notes

Prose and poems with endnotes were written using the following sources, either quoted verbatim or paraphrased.

[1] *Witness: Juárez.* HBO Documentary Films. Blue Light Media/Little Puppet Production. 2012

[2] Bowden, Charles. "The Sicario." *Harper's.* May, 2009.

[3] Rojo, Javier and Manuel Perez-Rocha. "NAFTA at 20: The New Spin." *Foreign Policy in Focus.* March 14, 2013. http://fpif.org/nafta_at_20_the_new_spin/

[4] https://groups.google.com/forum/#!searchin/frontera-list/murder$20rate$202011/frontera-list/B3zpbnw6RFE/tlZ13nA6XWIJ

[5] Knowledge. "Hispanic." Urban Dictionary. January 17, 2005. Last accessed November 2014. http://www.urbandictionary.com/define.php?term=Hispanic

[6] McGahan, Jason. "To Kill a Journalist." *Texas Observer.* January 24, 2013 http://www.texasobserver.org/to-kill-a-journalist

[7] Bowden, Charles. *Murder City: Ciudad Juarez and the Global Economy's New Killing Fields.* New York: Nation Books, 2011. p. 146

[8] Buggs. "CDG Hangs two Young Girls with Message to Z." *Borderland Beat.* November 2013. http://www.borderlandbeat.com/2013/11/cds-hangs-to-young-girls-with-message.html

[9] http://www.csmonitor.com/World/Americas/Latin-America-Monitor/2013/0718/Cold-case-98-percent-of-Mexico-s-2012-murder-cases-unsolved

[10] "The Mexican Undead: Toward a New History of the 'Drug War' Killing Fields." Molly Molloy, August 2013

[11] Molloy, Molly. "6 people killed yesterday in Juarez; 4 of the victims are women." Her commentary on the death toll for April 16, 2012 in frontera-list. http://fronteralist.org/2012/04/17/6-people-killed-yesterday-in-juarez-4-of-the-victims-are-women-2/

[12] http://adamjones.freeservers.com/juarez.htm

[13] Bowden, Charles and Molly Molloy. *El Sicario.*

[14] http://adamjones.freeservers.com/juarez.htm

[15] "Protocolo de Comunicación." *La Fiscalía.* A report on the Baseball Massacre in Valle de Juarez. From fronteralist.org. September 23, 2013.

[16] Ovemex. "Human Heads Left with the Ingredients Needed to Make Mexican Stew." *Borderland Beat.* March 7, 2011. http://www.borderlandbeat.com/2011/03/human-heads-left-with-ingredients-used.html

Garcia, Pat. "Arrested Mexican man confessed to have 'dissolved' 300 bodies." *NowPublic*. January 24, 2009. http://www.nowpublic. com/world/arrested-mexican-man-confessed-have-dissolved-300-bodies

"El pozole, 'El pozolero' y el término 'pozolear'." *narco popular*. February 5, 2009. http://narcopopular.wordpress.com/2009/02/05/el-pozole-el-pozolero-y-el-termino-pozolear/

Longmire, Sylvia. *Cartel: the Coming Invasion of Mexico's Drug Wars*. New York: Palgrave MacMillan, 2011. p. 33

[17] Discussion thread. "List of Juarez and Chihuahua State Femicide Victims." Crimeseekers. February 1, 2010. Last accessed February 10, 2014. http://crimeseekers.net/forums/showthread.php?5767-List-Of-Juarez-amp-Chihuahua-State-Femicide-Victims

[18] Nieto, Sandra Rodríguez. "I never imagined that they would kill them this way...." Translated by Molly Molloy. *El Diario de Juárez*. August 1, 2009. https://groups.google.com/forum/#!msg/frontera-list/i71QADlhU84/zo2LGR1DdOYJ

[19] Funari, Vicky and Sergio De La Torre. *Maquilopolis*. California News reel. 2006

[20] http://www.hanes.com/
http://www.zappos.com/smartwool-microweight-hiphugger
http://www.fruitoftheloom.com/
http://www.soma.com/
http://shop.cosabella.com/

[21] Landau, Saul and Argulo, Sonia. *Maquila: A Tale of Two Mexicos*. Cinema Guild; New York. 2000.

[22] The Borderplex Alliance. "Maquiladora FAQ." REDCO. El Paso Regional Economic Development Corporation. June 2013. <http://www.elpasoredco.org/regional-data/ciudad-juarez/twin-plant/maquiladora-faq>

[23] Paul, Christopher, Agnes G. Shaefer, and Colin P. Clarke. *The Challenge of Violent Drug-Trafficking Organizations: An Assessment of Mexican Security Based on Existing RAND Research on Urban Unrest, Insurgency, and Defense-Sector Reform*. Santa Monica, CA: RAND, 2011. pp. 2, 46

[24] From Borunda, Daniel. "2 mutilated bodies found in Juárez, 11 killed in mountain gunfight." *El Paso Times*. 9-29-14

[25] Borunda, Daniel. "Juárez shooting stops traffic at Bridge of the Americas." *El Paso Times*. October 26, 2010. http://www.elpasotimes.com/juarez/ci_16438601?source=pkg
Gómez Licón, Adriana. "3 men killed in Juárez near Bridge of the Americas were police." *El Paso Times*. October 27, 2010. http://www.elpasotimes.com/newupdated/ci_16447702

[26] Rodriguez, Sandra. "Mother of massacred students shakes up meeting." Translated by Molly Molloy. El Diario mx. February 12, 2010. https://groups.google.com/forum/#!msg/frontera-list/nACfSh-Akeo/h33QMS-o0HUJ

[27] From my notes taken during a Q and A session with Forrest Gander at New Mexico State University. November 15, 2013.

28 http://www.theguardian.com/world/2014/nov/09/protesters-fire-mexican-palace-anger-missing-students-grows?CMP=ema_565

29 Staley, James. "NMSU police continue to investigate burned body; autopsy necessary to determine ID and cause of death (update)." *Las Cruces Sun News*. January 28, 2014. http://www.lcsun-news.com/las_cruces-news/ci_25008358/portion-triviz-close-while-nmsu-burned-body-investigation

30 Archibold, Randall C. "El Chapo, Most-Wanted Drug Lord, Is Captured in Mexico." *The New York Times*. February 22, 2014. http://www.nytimes.com/2014/02/23/world/americas/joaquin-guzman-loera-sinaloa-drug-cartel-leader-is-captured-in-mexico.html?_r=0

31 Orquiz, Martin. "Cimbran a Juárez 25 masacres en cinco años." *El Diario mx*. September 24, 2009. http://diario.mx/Local/2013-09-24_cc3b99cc/cimbran-a-juarez-25-masacres-en-cinco-anos/

About the Author

Ed O'Casey earned an MA at the University of North Texas and an MFA at New Mexico State University. His poems have appeared in *Berkeley Poetry Review*, *Cold Mountain Review*, *Tulane Review*, *pacificRE-VIEW*, *Euphony*, *Poetry Quarterly*, *Whiskey Island*, *NANO Fiction*, and *West Trade Review*. He lives in northern Wisconsin.